5

Easy Steps

to

Homeschooling

H.D. Nelson

5
EASY STEPS TO
Homeschooling

HEATHER D. NELSON

H.D. Nelson

Copyright © 2020 Heather D. Nelson

All rights reserved.

All rights reserved. No part of this publication may be reproduced, distributed, or transmitted in any form or by any means, including photocopying, recording, or other electronic or mechanical methods, without the prior written permission of the publisher, except in the case of brief quotations embodied in critical reviews and certain other noncommercial uses permitted by copyright law.

First Printing 2020

ISBN-13: 978-1-7355355-0-0

DEDICATION

First and foremost, this book is dedicated to my sons...my joy & privilege every day. Teaching you is one of the greatest adventures of my motherhood journey. Don't ever stop making me laugh, monkey face.

And to my husband for constant support and encouragement, especially in homeschooling...you are my rock.

To my homeschool tribe of bold power-moms who lift me up and encourage me on this wild ride of ours...you are always the boost I need when the days get long.

And as always...to Peanut...who inspired my great work.

I am blessed by each and every one of you in my life.
I love you all now and forever.

H.D. Nelson

TABLE OF CONTENTS

Dear Parent(s)	**1**
Myth vs. Fact	6
Homeschool: A History	**7**
John Holt	11
John Taylor Gatto	12
Dr. Raymond S. Moore	13
Why Homeschool Works	**17**
A Note Before We Begin	25
STEP 1: Define Your 'Why'	**26**
4 Questions to Shape Your Why Statement	30
STEP 2: Keep It Legal	**39**
A Note on Global Homeschooling	45
STEP 3: Plan Your Space	**46**
A Note on Balance	53
STEP 4: Find Your Tribe	**55**
STEP 5: Choose Curriculum	**62**
Traditional	66
Programmed	67
Online	68
Unit Study	69
Classical	70
A Note of Caution	71
FAQ's	**73**
Socialization	73
College	77
Work & Homeschool	80
Cost	85
Special Needs	90
Final Thoughts	**95**
Resources & Support	**97**

H.D. Nelson

DISCLAIMER:

I am not qualified to offer legal advice. The information contained within this book is based off of experience and opinion from years of experience as a homeschool parent. If you have specific questions on how to begin homeschooling within your community, please refer to the regulations and laws of your hometown, county, district, and state. Should legal matters arise, please consult qualified legal counsel.
Any affiliate links within this book might benefit me, the author, directly.

Thank you for purchasing, *5 Easy Steps to Homeschool*.
I hope you enjoy.

H.D. Nelson

There is no school equal to a decent home and no teacher equal to a virtuous parent.

- Gandhi

Dear Parent(s),

If you are reading this book with the trembling hands of a parent just daring to utter the words, 'we think we might homeschool this year'…you are my people. If you feel destined to homeschool, but the calling feels larger than life, and you are overwhelmed by all the possibilities and potential laid before you…you are my people. If you feel backed into a corner at the intersection of public health and private finances where homeschooling seems the only resolution to a problem you didn't ask for, and you are attempting to make the best of things despite your better judgment…you are my people. If you previously considered homeschoolers to be weird and loathed the day you would ever find yourself on the sideline of home education to avoid the yellow bus…you are my tribe.

You see, I too would have once said that I would never, ever, ever, homeschool. I mistakenly thought homeschoolers were odd and antisocial. I had met homeschool children that seemed not to fit any mold my limited mind could create, and as a parent, I was myself raised in the public-school system. I envisioned the first emotion-filled day of school as a personal rite of passage. I just knew my first tear-filled day of kindergarten with my angelic firstborn would be memorialized by all those adorable pictures to flood my social media page for years to come. I would be room mom, class chaperone, well known and loved by all the faculty for my tireless spirit of helpfulness, and yes, I would eventually run the PTA like-a-mother. I was not only expecting to be a public-school parent; I looked FORWARD to being a public-school parent, complete with busy schedules, taxicab living, award shows, field trips, supply shopping, and more. I couldn't wait.

Then life changed.

My world went sideways, and suddenly public school just wasn't the best option for my family. It still was an option, to be clear, but it was no longer the best option. And in my scrambling to find any possible combination to make compulsory schooling work for my family, it became apparent that homeschooling was just the better fit. I talked to everyone, researched everything, and finally dared to voice my concerns to my husband whose wholehearted (and a little too fast) agreement caught me off-guard. It turned out he had the same concerns and was hoping I would feel the same way he did. I was never more terrified to have his full support than when we took that brave first step into a world I had never considered beforehand.

If you are reading this saying, "ME TOO," you…are my people.

I want it on record that my choice to homeschool was never about a feeling of deficit against public schools or the teachers/administrators who make them work. I have nothing but full respect for teachers, principals, administrators, lunch-ladies, janitors, bus drivers, the works. Teaching kids is hard. Teaching them en masse with federal mandates and funding to consider along with flu season, a shortage of substitutes, and a class full of shining bright faces who may or may not have had too much sugar for breakfast, is harder still. I have zero doubts that should we have chosen to place our kids in school, we would have had a mighty village, supported by a fantastic set of people, working hard to make it work. So, anyone who believes this book is a laundry list of complaints about the current school system might as well close the book, donate it to someone who needs it, and move along. You won't find that here.

This book isn't about them…this book is about you.

You have dipped your toe into the wide world of homeschooling and are beginning your journey into a life you may or may not have planned. If you are excited and eager and ready to dive in, I welcome you. I can't wait to see how your journey goes. But, if you are mystified, stupefied, overwhelmed, terrified, and completely perplexed on how even to begin homeschooling, I'm here for you. I welcome you with open arms, and an open book, to help share all my knowledge with you now and tell you unequivocally that yes, you can.

> You *can* homeschool your child.
> You *are* capable enough.
> They can *learn* from you.
> They can *thrive* like this.
> It doesn't have to be *perfect*.
> It doesn't have to be *pretty*.

Kudos to you for taking this step to learn all you can to start strong. Now sit down, grab a cup of coffee, and let's get started, shall we?

Signed,
Former Hesitant Homeschooler & Your Biggest Cheerleader
H.

Myth vs. Fact

Before we jump too deeply into the nuances of how to homeschool, I want to take a brief moment to dispel a few myths and preconceived notions that seem to be significant hurdles for a lot of hesitant homeschoolers. I want to help you set aside these notions so you can focus on the real question at hand.

I know that might seem counterintuitive to delay getting into the first step of a book entitled, *5 Easy Steps to Homeschooling*, but trust me…this is worth it. It's a quick read, but packed with important information, so stick with me. You won't regret it.

Homeschooling: A History

The first myth I want to address is that homeschooling is somehow new or novel. If you take even a fraction of time to investigate the history of education, you will see in almost all cultures across the globe, home education of children was the standard practice. The engagement of professional tutors was only available to the extremely wealthy or to royalty.

Even the idyllic scenes of the one-room[1] school-houses as the birthplace of modern-day public schooling is quickly stripped away when you realize how the 19th and early 20th-century structures were modeled. One teacher would unite all the students in the area, regardless of skill-level, gender, or age. In a single

---

[1] https://en.wikipedia.org/wiki/One-room_school#United_States

room, students would learn the basics: reading, writing, arithmetic, life skills, and the like. The teacher would modify the work as needed to accommodate age or learning obstacles, and when school was finished, the building served the community's needs as a chapel on Sundays or a meeting places for town gatherings. Upon digging deeper, it would appear those one-room schoolhouses weren't the beginning of current public school, but rather an extension of the home education model as was standard at the time.

This leads me to the second myth I want to dispel; the current model of compulsory education via large classrooms was never designed to be an ideal learning environment. It was designed for mass production and control.

Horace Mann[2], a Whig politician and lawyer who admired the efficiency of large industrial factories, argued that schools should be run in independent buildings like efficient factories. He believed this would transform unruly children into disciplined,

---

[2] *https://en.wikipedia.org/wiki/Horace_Mann*

judicious citizens. In fact, he believed it so strongly that, after accepting his position on the newly created Massachusetts Board of Education in 1837, he left all political ambitions behind and threw his energy into conventions, lectures, and correspondence introducing numerous reforms to legislate tax-supported public education and the feminization of the teaching force as modeled by the Prussian education system. Mann had bold merit to his efforts, to make education reachable for all socio-economic backgrounds, but his approach was flawed as it limited learning to happen within a box. A setup that could not have foreseen how much America would grow. With political supporters behind his efforts, it didn't take long before states began adopting variations of his system. The compulsory education laws that followed were equally effective, and by the 1970s an estimated 87% of kids were enrolled in public schools. And yet, homeschool was not gone.

A growing disenchantment with the secularization of public education lead to a rise in families who kept their children home to educate in a way that fit their family values. The birth of the modern American homeschool movement you know of today really wasn't a birth but rather a rebirth. The fathers of the modern movement are said to be John Holt, John Taylor Gatto, and Raymond Moore; each of which opposed this large schoolroom approach for one reason or another.

John Holt

John Holt was an American author and educator who lived from 1923-1985. He began his career teaching elementary school in the early 50s, but by the 60s had already grown disillusioned with the system. He penned his first book, *How Children Fail*[3], in 1964 and followed it with, *How Children Learn*[4], in 1967. He is often referred to as the father of the unschooling movement. While I'm not a huge fan of the unschooling concept, I do agree with his tenant that children love to learn but often hate *the manner* in which they are being taught.

Holt sincerely believed that the growing trend in public schools to encourage *correct* answers left little room for children to see any value in thinking, discovery, and understanding along the way of learning. He feared that if a change did not occur, children would lose the ability to overcome challenges because of an inability to problem solve without fear of punishment. Holt pursued the

---

[3] Holt, John (1964). *How Children Fail* ISBN-10 0201484021

[4] Holt, John (1964). *How Children Learn* ISBN-10 9780738220086

awareness of his beliefs with a fierce tenacity up until his death. His final book was published posthumously in 1989 entitled, *Learning All the Time*[5], and is still in circulation today.

John Taylor Gatto

John Taylor Gatto,[6] was another American author[7] and school teacher who lived from 1935-2018. His public-school teaching career was longer than Holt's, and he was the recipient of several prestigious teaching awards, including New York City Teacher of the Year in 1989, 1990, and 1991. He also won New York State Teacher of the Year in 1991. His official retirement letter was submitted as an op-ed to the Wall Street Journal. The letter was so widely read that it launched not only his retirement, but his new career in public speaking and writing about the glories of homeschooling and open-source learning.

---

[5] Holt, John (1989). *Learning All The Time* ISBN-10 0201550911

[6] https://en.wikipedia.org/wiki/John_Taylor_Gatto

[7] Gatto, John Taylor (2017) *Dumbing Us Down* ISBN-10 0865718547

In his much-reviewed paper entitled *The Exhausted School* published in 1993, Gatto made a straightforward statement that I adore. He said, "It is not the fault of bad teachers, or of too little money spent. Structurally, schools fly in the face of how children learn." Gatto believed fervently that the current public-school system grew from the captains of industry who wanted an educational system that would maintain a social order by teaching only the information to support the socio-political order with little room to grow and change and learn.

Up until his death in 2018, John Taylor Gatto educated others by exposing the origins of what he believed to be a government monopoly on compulsory education. Again, for him it wasn't about the teachers, but the system within which they had to work that was the problem.

Dr. Raymond S. Moore

Dr. Raymond S. Moore was the one who, I believe, turned our modern homeschooling movement on its ear. In 1972, California was considering a new law to make school compulsory for children as young as two years old. Dr. Raymond S. Moore poured his entire educational career (as a teacher, principal, superintendent of California public schools, and Ph.D. in Education) into researching the effects of compulsory schooling on young children. His findings steered his career away from public school education and into homeschooling support. He submitted an article to Harper's that became so widely read that Reader's Digest requested a whole book on the topic. From that point on, Dr. Moore worked tirelessly with legislative bodies to establish legal precedents for parents desiring to homeschool.

His philosophy was one I can definitely get behind, which is why I love his approach so much. He believed, as I do, that children need *individualized* attention in the early years. In his book *The Successful Homeschool Family Handbook*[8], he shares that schooling should be an easy-to-live-with family adventure. Dr. Moore believed that kids needed educational endeavors, free from

---

[8] Moore, Raymond S. (1994) *The Successful Homeschool Family Handbook*
ISBN-10 0785281754

the pressure to perform. He felt that later in life, success would come on the heels of early *individualized* attention, thus allowing children to mature at their own rate. By encouraging exploration and diligence first, later academics would thrive. Before his death, he established his unique educational approach known as the Moore Formula[9] and his foundation continues to this day.

Personally, I boil all this down into my own belief system.

> Children should embrace the *act* of learning, just as much as they embrace the *facts* they're learning.

Each of these men (and countless others like them) saw holes from within the system and set themselves to the task of forging something different. If that sounds familiar to you, well, it could be because that is the same approach many homeschool families work from even now.

---

[9] The Moore Foundation *https://www.moorefoundation.com/*

The last compulsory attendance law was passed by Mississippi in 1918.[10] If you do the math, at the original publication of this book in 2020, that is just over 100 years ago.[11] In the great, grand, history of our world, one-hundred years is not that old! You looking at a new approach for your child's education is actually you embracing the next natural step in your ever-evolving role of parenthood. You are in very good company!

---

[10] Katz, Michael S. *A History of Compulsory Education Laws* (PDF). *ERIC - Institute of Education Sciences*. ERIC.

[11] *https://en.wikipedia.org/wiki/Homeschooling#History*

Why
HOMESCHOOL WORKS

Allow me to be bold for a moment and state my honest opinion. Homeschooling works. I know that seems like an oversimplification, but there it is. The broader statement isn't *just* that I believe homeschool works, but rather *why* I think homeschool works.

Homeschool works because it is a
natural extension of parenting.

Given the heated nature surrounding the political interest in parental rights and freedoms in our country today, this small statement can't be emphasized enough. So, I'll repeat it. Homeschooling is a *natural extension* of parenting. We parents start from day one, learning as we go. We aren't formally educated in a classroom setting for 12 years on the nuances of diapers, bottles, and swaddling before we are sent home with a tiny, frail creature to raise. We are not tested, quizzed, and graded on our ability to tie shoes, sing ABCs, and coax the nap time of a 2-year-old who refuses to lay down. We aren't asked to show a medical degree before we care for fevers, vomit, chicken-pox, and other childhood calamities.

We teach them to tie their shoes because we first learned to tie our own. We teach them to drive a car because we first learned to drive one ourselves. Should our child encounter some struggle we have not experienced personally, we are encouraged to use any number of resources made available to educate, advocate, and empower ourselves. Why is there a preconceived notion that if we lack a Master's in Early Childhood Education, that we are not qualified to teach our children to read, write, calculate math, create art, play music, and more? Educating your child happens in a series of natural baby-steps that quite literally is an extension of what you already do.

Your baby is born, and you care for them. As they learn to crawl, you make the space safe and encourage them to explore. When your baby begins to babble, you engage in conversation in anticipation of those first words. They walk and run and talk, and you follow and chase and join in at every step. You teach them colors, shapes, numbers, their ABCs and even how to tie their shoes. That's a breath away from them mimicking things you do every day like cooking, running, gaming, or singing. Don't look now, but that's homeschooling!

Deciding to lead your child's formal education may be different than what you anticipated, but you are capable. The amount of curriculum and resources out there is astonishing. You are already, no doubt, adept at not only seeing what your kids enjoy but researching and filtering the amount of information they see/hear to make sure what they are getting is good quality. You will apply those same parenting skills when choosing learning materials. You already know your child enough to know what they like and don't like, and you will use that to help them select electives. No doubt, you have already implemented things to accommodate your child's safe raising, and you will simply expand on that space now to give them room to spread those intellectual wings to include things like reading books, creating art, and blowing things up for science. Will there by a slight learning curve while you all figure out how this looks? Sure. But homeschooling has always worked because it's a very natural state of being for families.

But there is more to my idyllic outlook on homeschooling than the warm and fuzzy feelings. Homeschooling also works because it's convenient, adaptable, specialized, and limitless. Anything your child wishes to learn is at their fingertips. Any struggles, challenges, disorders, or hurdles you encounter will have resources available to you as well. Who *better* to advocate for your child's educational needs than the parent who loves them most? No more setting alarms and dragging exhausted kiddos out of bed to catch that morning bus. Homeschool can now start at whatever time best suits your family's natural circadian rhythms. Say goodbye to 2+ hours of homework every night before dinner, and say hello to family evenings spent in family time. Want a different style of instruction than what is offered in a group environment? Welcome to the flexibility of implementing any method that suits your child best.

Homeschooling also works because of the long-term educational value. As of the date of this publication, there are approximately 2.5 million homeschool students in the United States. While that makes up only 3-5% of the school-age children in America, it has grown anywhere from 2-8% per annum over the past few years. Personally, I suspect the 2020-2021 school year will see a HUGE boom in homeschooling due to the concerns of the Covid-19, but I digress. According to the National Home Education Research Institute[12], homeschooling families represent a savings of nearly $27 billion taxpayer dollars due to the school programs they do not utilize. They also found that home-educated children scored 15-30% higher[13] on standardized testing regardless

---

[12] National Home Education Research Institute - Research Facts on Homeschooling circa 2020 - *https://www.nheri.org/research-facts-on-homeschooling/*

[13] *Academic achievement and demographic traits of homeschool students: A nationwide study*, Brian D. Ray, 2010, *Academic Leadership Journal*

of their parent's level of formal education. SAT and ACT scores land above average so often that universities now actively recruit homeschool students at the high school level via online distance learning programs.

I won't sugarcoat things beyond the realistic. There are stories of failure within the homeschooling community. It's not always perfect, but the same is true in public school. It would be foolish to think one bad example writes-off an entire educational approach; thus, I return to my initial sentiment: Homeschool works because educating children at home is natural.

The other major reason, I believe, that homeschool works is one not many people share with new families.

> In homeschooling, parents learn right alongside their children.

As children embrace their early education years, parents brush-up on basics they'd long forgotten. When the kids explore a new curiosity or passion, the parents get to explore along with them. Art, music, programming, architecture, invention, science, mathematics, and more are now available to both parent *and child*! This beautiful, symbiotic relationship between parenting and education creates limitless opportunities for educational exploration unlike anything else.

Embracing the truth that homeschool is neither novel nor unique, and adding the acceptance that homeschooling is a natural extension of parenting, I go back to the question from the start. Should you homeschool your child? For me, the answer was easy. I saw a gap in what public school options could provide and I was *called* to homeschool. Empowered, passionate, and instantly committed.

So, ask yourself the following:

1. Do the public/private school options in your area fit the bill for your child's individual needs (educational/physical/emotional)?
2. Do you feel that the public/private school values being taught in your area fit your family's values?
3. Is the public/private school schedule (days in school/hours per day/days-off/etc.) in keeping within your family culture?
4. Are you comfortable with the teacher assigned to your child being the primary caregiver and influencer of your child five days a week?

If the answer to any of the above questions is "NO," then perhaps homeschooling is something you should consider.

A note before we begin.

In the spirit of full disclosure, I will share that I am just now finishing my 5th year of homeschooling. I came right out of the gate with 3 full-time homeschooling kiddos. My oldest starting kindergarten and twin preschoolers!

Over the years, we have moved no less than three times, one of those being cross-country. I have had committed school rooms as well as shared spaces with the dining room table. From sitting in chairs to traveling around finishing assignments on the road, we've tried nearly everything. The early days were wonderfully exhausting but also incredibly enlightening.

My kids thrived, but I was the one having mind-blowing revelations. I learned about their styles and strengths, as well as my own. I learned how to fit homeschooling into our lives, and how to navigate the pitfalls. My experience inspires the following advice, which I feel is paramount for new families entering the homeschool arena.

Step 1:
DEFINE YOUR WHY

Some homeschool veterans advise that you should spend months meditating and praying on the entirety of your child's educational career. Shaping the entire 12-year plan into a mission statement, a vision board, and a signed family manifesto. They hope it will help you to stay laser-focused for the next 18 years with unshakable confidence from day one. To all that I say, HORSECRAPPERY!

Focusing too hard on the 20 year long-goal and weighing the eternal spiritual consequences and emotionally stable outcome of your child is *just* a touch too much. Are short- and long-term goals important? Yes. But don't get overwhelmed in them to the detriment of just getting started. Again, this book is for the new parent, just peeking behind the curtain of homeschooling for the first time. If you are a parent who wakes up in a cold sweat feeling confident that you want to homeschool but has no clue how to homeschool, I'm talking to you. The Brave, The Proud, The Terrified! Life changes at the speed of light sometimes, so to think you will sit down and create a master plan to last you for 18 years is just nuts. Let's start smaller and focus on only one year. Let's focus on your first year and make it a great one. Allow me to help you wipe away that cold sweat of panic and narrow down your emotion-filled indecision by focusing on this one question. Why do you want to homeschool?

One of the first questions you should be able to intelligently answer about your decision to educate your children at home is "Why." This will be the most common question you will encounter from the world at large, and spending time investing in a deep understanding of your motivations will help you navigate challenging times of doubt that every parent faces.

To help you answer this, I'm offering up a few starter questions on the next few pages. These are not meant to pin you down, but set you free. Let these guide your thought processes and don't feel burdened by them. No one will see your answers but you! Grab another cup of coffee and let's dig in.

4 Questions to Shape Your Why-Statement

1. **Why don't you want to use the Public school near you?** Understanding why you are steering away from the community school options in your area will help you more confidently address the nosy nay-sayers who judge you for being at the grocery store at 10 am on a Tuesday with your kids. Furthermore, your answer here could help drive your curriculum choices or even help you in scheduling out your days. And, be at peace. There is no wrong answer here. This is a personal preference for you and your family's unique needs. So be brutally honest with yourself.

2. **What are the benefits of homeschooling your *child*?** Beyond wanting to bypass the community school options around you, for homeschooling to work you must believe in its potential for your child. Home education, like anything else in parenting, takes sacrifice and commitment. Both of those are easier done if you find true worth in what you are doing. Be detailed and list off every benefit to your child that you can think of here.

3. **Why do you think homeschooling is best for your *family*?** Homeschooling your child will shift the culture of your whole family. As such, you need to think about all the pieces of your life. Think about work schedules, special needs, traditions, budgeting, and more. Mentally sift through a standard week or month or even year and think about how homeschooling will affect each situation. This will be unique to your family culture. The considerations of your neighbor won't be the same since you have a different family.
4. **What beliefs do you feel are served homeschooling?** Now I'm going to be a little harsh here, but YOU MUST BE SPECIFIC! If it's a religious choice, then point to the specific book of scripture that drives you. If it's a secular morality choice, then point to the particular character trait or worldview. Homeschooling is a brilliant opportunity to double-down on the family values. Your kids will be free of doctrine(s) taught in the school systems for better or worse. It is up to you to make sure you raise kids with the convictions you want them to learn. Don't slack, don't sugar coat, and don't back down here. Be raw and honest with yourself.

If you aren't totally hating my guts for making you dig deep on those, allow me now to explain how these questions shaped my own *Why Statement*. Moreover, how my *Why* has shielded me during times of doubt and criticism.

I used the same four questions I posed to you and answered them for myself in detail. I was able to write down that I have a child with three auto-immune conditions. The public-school system around us was excellent, but the class sizes were large, and the days were long. Those poor teachers were undoubtedly working hard for each and every child, but they had limitations. The combination of long days and health challenges made for a less than ideal dynamic for my son. Add to that our family juggles many doctor appointments, medical bills/budget needs, and my husband works long hours. As such, we felt homeschooling would allow us to both educate our kids but also allow for flexibility to accommodate the often wildly unpredictable nature of my son's health needs.

Homeschooling has allowed for a conducive and consistent foundation for our kids despite the ever-changing tides we live within. My goal was, and is, to help our kids find balance and still raise men of integrity and character who I can launch into the world with confidence.

Once *you* have completed your personal inventory here, take a step back, and really look at your answers. Maybe take the day or even the week to think on them, there is no need to rush here. Discuss it with your spouse or a trusted friend and come back fresh to see if your answers need to be changed. If your answers slant towards the negative, I encourage you to revise them. The more positive you can make your answers, the more positive of an outlook as a whole that you will have about homeschooling in general. That will bleed over through the years to your kids who will have a positive outlook about being homeschooled too.

For example, if you are using a loathing of the local school as your primary motivator…your gauge is broken…please try again. Flawed and imperfect as they may be, our school systems and the teachers within them are warriors who deserve respect for their hard work. You don't want your children living in fear of public school, nor do you want your friends or family members who choose public school, to think you feel they are inferior parents.

Keep your why statement positive. Notice I did NOT criticize or shine a negative light on school nurses or teacher training or anything of the sort. However, I stated the facts of our situation and how I felt they didn't fit what our kid needed. Our decision was about doing what is best for our family. In truth, you don't know what the future will bring, and you may need that same community school system at some point.

> You choosing to homeschool isn't about *them*; it's about **you**.

Once you have revised your four answers, start trimming the fat. Your goal is a quick elevator pitch. Later, if you feel called, you can create a mission statement to be laminated and bound in a 3-ring binder. Today, I want to help you confidently spout off your answer with ease.

I was able to take my entire reason for homeschooling, and trim it down to a simple 3-sentence statement. I can now rattle off my *Why Statement* at the grocery store to a nosy passerby in under 5 seconds. I don't feel compelled to unpack the layers upon layers of medical knowledge in my brain to justify my choice. I don't need to get into the nuances of classroom sizes or hours in the day or any other information I used to build my answer. I just pull my quick statement out of my pocket and let it hang. Between my swift response, and my confidence in responding I rarely get push back! My elevator-pitch *Why* is as follows:

> *One of my sons has three autoimmune conditions, one of which is a complex form of Type 1 Diabetes. Homeschooling allows us to balance his health requirements with the fun and exciting educational opportunities my kids deserve.*
> *It's a perfect fit for us!*

In three short sentences, I addressed the question at hand, shared my inarguable reason, and swung for the fences with a positive close that leaves zero openings for debate. The best part of my *Why Statement* is that it's remained largely unchanged over the years. On days when nosy questions get on my last nerve, my answer is unchanging. When I'm exhausted, and the well-meaning family pulls the *'why don't you just put them in school'* crap, my answer is the same. When I, myself, am tired and strung out and feeling the burden of it all wondering how I'll get through another day, week, MONTH…my answer spurs me on. Because the VERY core truth to this whole practice is this:

A good *Why* will ALWAYS drive your **How**.

When you are motivated beyond yourself, you find the path to continue no matter the fatigue or struggles or frustrations you come upon. And should your *Why* change, you will have full confidence that you are making a solid decision yet again to meet the needs of your family during a new season of life.

So, create your *Why Statement*, my new homeschooling friend, and embrace the journey. Each homeschool year ahead of you will bring new changes, both good and bad. You will learn an immense amount of stuff about yourself as a parent, an educator, and a multi-tasking ninja! You will learn a ton about your kids, too. They have their own learning styles, their own struggles, their own interests. Homeschooling can be fun for the whole family, so don't get too overwhelmed worrying about the results of their high school SATs when they are just entering elementary years. Let us survive our first year of homeschooling first. Better yet, let's *thrive*.

Step 2:
KEEP IT LEGAL

If you have made it to step 2, pat yourself on the back. You've done some serious soul searching and are well motivated to continue the journey to home education. Good on you for making time for introspection! You have undoubtedly increased your self-awareness a notch or two and are now more confident than before in your decision. Now we roll up our sleeves and begin the important work of setting yourself up for maximum success, and that starts with taking necessary steps to ensure you are educating within the bounds of the law.

If I had a nickel every time someone asked me if homeschooling was legal, I'd be so rich I wouldn't be writing books for a living. A parent's right to educate their child is not only natural but federally protected in America. That said, the U.S. recognizes state sovereignty. As such, each state[14] has its own regulations to follow to ensure that your efforts remain within parameters of what is allowed. The boundaries you need to work within can vary from state to state. In some states, parents have no restrictions whatsoever. In contrast, other states require parents to educate their children under what's called an Umbrella School[15].

Some states require notification of your intent to homeschool. While some states want a one-time notification, others request annual renewal notices. Whatever level of detail or repetition your state requires; the general notification is usually not complicated. Most notices are submitted to the state department of education, but some states leave the administration handled down at the county, city, or even district levels. Most data stays at the local level. Whatever your state requires, you must comply to move forward. Type up your form letter (many examples of which can

---

[14] Homeschool State Laws. *https://homeschoolstatelaws.com/*

[15] *Umbrella Schools* oversee State legal mandates while still affording parents the freedom to choose homeschooling that fits their family's needs.

be found online) and save it for reuse year after year. Set a calendar reminder in your planner, phone, or computer for annual notification dates and move forward.

You might be asked to show your credentials for teaching, with a few states requiring you to meet specific educational qualifications beyond being "competent" or "capable of teaching." Some states want a high school diploma or GED, but a few states want to see proof of accredited college credits or completion of an in-home study program. A few states mandate a criminal background check that would disqualify a parent from home education in the event of a criminal record. Specifically, a history of child abuse/endangerment, sexual offenses, or any crimes that would also disqualify them from employment as a public-school teacher. If a background check is required, you will be notified of when and how to complete it.

Curriculum mandates are another area that new homeschool families need to research. A good portion of states have testing and assessment requirements of some sort. That can be quarterly or annual standardized testing at a facility of the state's choosing, or simply a need to mail in the results of standardized testing completed in the home. There are also requirements in a few states where they require homeschooling families to provide instruction on a particular list of subjects (while still giving you the freedom to choose how you meet that need). Usually, these same states also have a "term" requirement that asks parents to track and report on attendance to ensure they meet a minimum days-in-school metric. These requests usually aren't restrictive, but being aware of them from the beginning helps you be prepared to put systems in place to keep your homeschool efforts rolling forward.

While most states don't require record-keeping of academic progress, there are very few states requiring parents to maintain portfolios, track attendance, report immunizations, and more. Some of these records are kept on file at the local level, while others report up to the state legislative body. Whether through original reporting or an umbrella school, most of the time, this is simply a matter of good record-keeping and, again, putting proper processes in place. Finding out your local and state laws is essential, and number 2 in my steps to help you *start* as you mean to go.

You can do an individual state by state search to find out what you need to comply. Likewise, you can find an organization that compiles the data for you. One example of this is the Homeschool Legal Defense Association[16]. Founded in the early 1980s by attorney and homeschooling parent Mike Farris, the HSLDA started with the goal of making homeschooling possible for everyone through advocacy. They even provide a state by state[17] listing on the legal requirements to homeschool across the U.S. They are just one of the many wonderful organizations out there that offer information, education, and encouragement for families seeking to homeschool their children. Knowing your state requirements is a burden that falls to you as the parent to educate yourself on, but the information is readily available and in almost all cases it's simply a matter of knowing what steps you need to

---

[16] Homeschool Legal Defense Association - https://hslda.org/legal/

[17] *Homeschool Laws by State or Territory*. HSLDA (2020)

check-off each year. Once you have a firm grasp on what your requirements are, you are ready for step 3!

A Note on Global Homeschooling

For my global homeschoolers at large, different countries have different requirements. Some are like the U.S. with individual territories regulating unique guidelines (like Australia and Canada). Other countries require regular national-level registration and reporting, and others still have outlawed homeschooling altogether.

I encourage you to research your requirements to ensure you are well within the measure of the law where you live. The same is true for my brave U.S. military families who homeschool while being transported around the world in service to our country. I can't write a book for every country, but I'm with you in spirit.

Step 3:
PLAN YOUR SPACE

I love homeschooling, and I've done so in a multitude of places and spaces. As such, I'm flexible to whatever home our life brings us to. I even get a little giddy talking about homeschool space...now. However, I confess that before my first year, I was utterly freaked out and, as such, went entirely overboard in my preparations.

I've learned so much from then until now. I still get a little rush every year thinking about rearranging, decorating, planning, etc. It's almost like revisiting the precious nesting phase from pregnancy days. I see our homeschool space as a blank slate of potential, and I get all warm and fuzzy thinking of the time we'll spend in there. But please note the small word I used in the previous sentence; *space*.

You don't need an entire school-building to educate your children. You do not need a whole schoolroom to teach your children. All you need is a little space, that's all. It can be 100% dedicated to school space, or it can be a transient spot like the kitchen table that transforms daily to meet the need. Remove the idea that it must look like a schoolroom and embrace the freedom of homeschooling by choosing any space in your house that fits what your family has available. You don't need to move into a different house or start knocking down walls.

> You do not need to renovate to educate!

Whether you are working from a tiny one-bedroom house or have a huge empty loft begging for blackboards, you can educate your child at home. I have met friends who lived in a small apartment of less than 1000 square feet who homeschooled their kids at the breakfast bar. I myself have had both dedicated school rooms and shared dining room space in somebody else's house.

Wherever you are living right now, you can make space for homeschooling.

Take a moment to evaluate where you live, what area you have, and rearrange it to make a dedicated spot (even if that dedicated spot is transient and changes places for mealtimes). Consider lighting, electrical outlets, and ample work surface for your kid(s) to sit. Once you have selected the best place, you have available to you and take a moment to make it a clean slate. Remove anything unessential to the area. Be vicious and declutter that area like Marie Kondo[18] herself was coming for an inspection! Strip the space as bare as you can to give your eyes a chance to visualize its repurposed potential. After that it's a simple matter of organization.

You've heard the old adage, 'a place for everything and everything in its place.' That is true with homeschool as in everything else. You will collect all manner of items as you move forward with home education, and those items will need a home.

---

[18] Kondo, Marie (2014) - Author of *"Life Changing Magic of Tidying Up."*

You'll need some basic organization. Bookshelves, baskets, or over the door holders, there are no limitations to the options out there for organizing your new school space. It can be simple tubs tucked under a cabinet or a series of binders that line up on a shelf. Try and think of what you need to have your items stored away.

Some people might invite you to hit-up that popular visual search engine for inspiration. Frankly, I find that kind of searching a black hole of lost time where I lose hours of my life only to come out with a deep need to craft a pencil-shaped 3-tiered tape-dispensing organizer with decoupaged pictures of my children that doubles as a beer-cozy with built-in hand warmers. Please…just stop.

Don't let yourself be drawn to the sparkly newness of it all, like I once was. Think basics. Your child needs a place to sit, and supplies to work. If you see a need, then keep it simple and utilize the glorious helpers over at Amazon[19]. It would help if you had a place to put crayons and pencils and maybe glue sticks. It's not

---

[19] *Amazon.com -*

rocket science, don't overthink it and don't blow your budget on it. If you can't find what you need for the right price online, visit your local dollar store. Teachers have held the dollar stores in their hip-pocket for years as a secret weapon for inexpensive school essentials, and it's an excellent place for a new homeschooler to look. They sometimes even have cute caddies to organize stuff if you need your homeschool space to transition throughout the day.

Whatever you decide on, avoid the office supply stores during back-to-school time. I made that mistake and bought four years of color-coded pencils to match my post-it notes. Don't go down that crazy road. Keep it minimalistic and accessible, so you have room to grow.

Once you have space and supply storage, make sure you have a workspace for your kid. Consider the age of your child and what you think would work best for them. After all, a 4 yr. old wiggly toddler won't need a full-on desk and swivel chair for a while, whereas a lanky teenager won't appreciate foam floor mats covered in the ABCs. This doesn't have to be more than your kitchen breakfast bar, but if you have space and need for an actual desk, you can find them cheap at Ikea, Amazon, Walmart, and more. I have purchased desks for as little as 25 bucks. I have also repurposed beanbags into a reading nook for 5-year-olds.

It doesn't have to be pricey to be effective, and you might have what you need right in your own house. Again, you are looking to make something minimalistic and inexpensive your first year, so you have room and resources to grow as your child's needs change. A lot of homeschoolers like the rolling drawer carts to help organize books/supplies and those also make for smooth transition spaces if your room is multipurpose. A straightforward bookshelf is all you need this first year, and even then, you can use the small modular cube systems and tuck them away in a closet.

Spend a few days setting up what you THINK will be a good educational space. But do it with a loose grip. Be prepared for ultimate flexibility, and don't be afraid to go outside your selected area. Your space at home is just a starting point; the beauty of homeschool is the room to spread your wings!

If you begin homeschooling and find your child unable to sit still for math, move math to the back porch. Do spelling drills on the trampoline. Memorize poetry over breakfast and complete science experiments in the garage. Remember, you homeschool. Home is the keyword. Anywhere in your house can and should be a space to learn. That principle extends beautifully to the car, on the road, in a library, or outdoors. The whole wide-world is waiting for you!

A Note on Balance

I would be remiss if I ended this chapter on carving out space for homeschooling without also addressing the need for mental/emotional space. Inevitably, homeschooling will demand a little more from you as a parent. You can be wholly successful at homeschooling, but that doesn't mean there won't be growing pains. Whether that means more demands on your daily time investment in the attention your child needs for education, or more demands on you mentally as you learn all the things you need to be homeschool-ready. There is a mental load to homeschooling that can't be understated, and thus you *must* make space for it.

Not only are you going to have a period of adjustment, but so will your child. Ease off the gas-pedal in other areas, so you have time to honor their emotions too. Give them time to relax, play, talk, or just be in the room with you. Kids don't often come with a set schedule for emotional processing, so make sure you have a little room in your life to be accessible when they do decide to get chatty.

During the first precious weeks/months of home education, try to keep your calendar clear so you have space for downtime. You can return to regular activities and a packed schedule after you have adjusted to this new normal, but you need to respect the process and give yourself a little breathing room.

Step 4:
FIND YOUR TRIBE

Just like any long-term commitment, homeschooling can come with the occasional side of burnout. For me, that moment hit about four years in. I had spent my first year figuring out what didn't work, then my second year discovering what did work. My third year brought fine-tuning to my schedule, and by year four, we'd fallen into a rhythm and made things work fairly seamlessly. Unfortunately, by four years in, we'd also moved three times, and I'd grown in and out of several support situations, including a year-long stint with virtually NO real-world connections. My kids thrived, but I was taking bottomless-drinks from a dry pool. I seriously considered ending homeschooling.

Of course, my well-done *Why Statement* hadn't changed, and I knew homeschooling was still a massive part of our life. So, I began to investigate what else was missing and low and behold, I lacked a tribe.

So many people worry that homeschool kids lack socialization, but the reality is, kids can fall off a log and make a friend. Homeschooling parents, on the other hand, can often struggle to make meaningful connections. We put on our blinders, trudge through our days, and by the time we come up for air, we are ready to fall into bed. It's no wonder many homeschool families who begin their home education journey end up feeling exhausted after a few months.

Finding your homeschool tribe is one of the most important things you can do for your well-being. Homeschooling can be challenging even on the best days. The early days can feel isolating and leave you pulling your hair out in frustration. A group of like-minded parents who let you vent, rant, or give you a soundboard and an ugly cry over a glass of wine, can keep you going.

> A word to the wise.
> The hive-mind is a double-edged sword, and you get the good with the bad.

Social media makes it super easy to find a group of like-minded parents in the virtual world. Open any social media app of choice and do a quick search for homeschool groups in your area. It might take a little trial and error to find a group you click with and feel comfortable interacting with, but it's work worth doing. Moreover, you can do it from home in your PJ's, so you have zero excuses not to do this.

These online groups and social media followings are ideal places to poll the hive mind and get a pulse on the local homeschool scene in your hometown. Have curriculum questions, or wondering how to get your child to do their daily reading? Ask online! Within minutes, all the well-meaning surrogate parents will flood your inbox with ideas, suggestions, links, lists, and cautionary tales. I have even found ways to save money on curriculum and supplies using the buddy-system and/or the selling of used materials. You simply must get online and start searching!

Use wisdom and discernment as you navigate relationships but enjoy the invaluable resources you now have access to when you need it.

In-person connections are where the real gold lies. Having a good friend or two who you can commiserate with over a cup of coffee while the kids hang out is life-giving. The challenge here can be finding the time to make connections and then investing the time in them to keep them healthy. You can start by reaching out to homeschoolers you already know (and yes, you likely know more of them than you realize). Ask to meet up for coffee or a mom's-night-out for dinner or drinks. See what common ground you have and try to find any commonalities with your kids or homeschooling. Try to plan for regular meet-ups. I love hosting a monthly homeschool Mom-2-Mom group, where we can all collaborate on topical discussions. They always start studiously enough but usually dissolve into puddles of laughter at the shared hi-jinx we get to enjoy. Honestly, by the end of them, I am reinvigorated and enamored with homeschooling once again.

You can look into a co-op. Co-ops are groups of homeschool families who collaborate on the educational initiatives of their children. Usually, they meet and work together to achieve common academic goals, centering the group activities around social arts, events, service work, or even educational presentations. If you are looking for some built-in structure and regular interaction each week, a co-op might be a fantastic option. If those feel too structured, embrace park days, playgroups, and even game cafes where kids meet-up to play. Likely there are parents in the wings that you can get to know during those times to make a few friends.

Having lived and homeschooled now in several places, I will attest that what makes the difference is the people, not the location. Building connections and having advocacy support groups are often the oxygen I need to reinvigorate myself during times I'm feeling depleted. It may take multiple tries with different groups over weeks or even months, but it is the most important thing you can do for yourself.

Reminder, in case you missed my point up top, your kids will fall off a log and make a friend; you do this work for *you*. Finding a tribe for yourself that feels natural and has opportunities your kids don't hate can be tricky, but it should be one of the paramount goals you set to help you make homeschooling a success.

Resist the urge to overschedule yourself like a cruise-line social director, conforming to every whim that passes by. Be selective and intentional about where you invest your energy, so you don't end up obligated to a group that doesn't feed your soul. Start small, and be genuine. This shouldn't feel like running the gauntlet to get a little face time.

Worst case scenario, say you genuinely try to find a local group, and there are none…not even one. You check out social media and search the internet, and there is no homeschool group in your hometown. Guess what that means, you get to start one. It's free, easy, and with a few clicks on the keyboard, you can be blasting away about a homeschool group for new homeschooling parents.

You will be shocked to find out how many other parents were out there and were just too afraid to take that leap. It might feel silly to be trying to make new friends, and you might even feel overwhelmed and think this is just too much to take on right now, but I can't say this enough. Find a person, or two or three, that energizes and supports you and wants to join you in your homeschool walk. Proceed with safety and caution to avoid the crazies but otherwise be brave and get out there.

Step 5:
CHOOSE CURRICULUM

Remember back in the history section of this book when I spoke of Horace Mann? That political guy in the Whig party who had an eye turned toward educational reform used his law background to great effect as we toured around advocating for his new system of education. During that time, he coined a great turn of phrase when he said education was "the great equalizer of the conditions of men - the balance-wheel of social machinery." I bring that up here because I have always believed a variation of this is valid within the homeschool community.

There are so many teaching styles and learning styles, and with them are multiple ways of combining them into a homeschooling approach. As such, no two homeschool families are exactly alike.

It's beautifully built to be that way, but some people worry that one method of schooling might be superior to another, and thus if you choose incorrectly, your kids could end up with a sub-par education. My answer to that worry is simple.

> Curriculum is the great equalizer in homeschooling.

What works for one set of kids might not be a great fit for your brood, but that's okay. Just as there is a multitude of methods for approaching home education, there is a multitude of curriculum options to complement those methods. If you are a multi-degreed professional, or a multi-tasking ninja rocking a high school diploma, there is a vast sea of educational materials to enhance all your natural abilities and fill in the gaps where your own knowledge might be a little thin.

Whether your family is financially comfortable or making that shoe-string sing at the end of each month, there are learning materials for every budget so your child has the educational opportunities they deserve. No matter what doubt, worry, or concern you might be wrestling with, chances are there is a curriculum to help fill that need. Hence my theory, curriculum is the great equalizer of homeschoolers.

Once you have defined your *Why Statement*, and researched the legal requirements, and assessed your space, you are ready to choose a curriculum! More often than not, this area is the stuff of flop-sweats for new homeschooling parents. They worry that they won't find a good curriculum or that they won't find an affordable curriculum. I hear concerns that they won't know how to teach the material, or that their kids won't know what to do with the curriculum: all very valid and understandable concerns but honestly all 100% unfounded.

Curriculum is one of the largest growing fields within the home-education industries. The number of resources is astounding and within them is nearly every nook-and-cranny of specialization you could want to fit even the *most* unique educational need. Whether you want a curriculum that is expensive and turn-key or free and minimalist, built for groups of multiple ages/stages or catered to individual learning disabilities, online or in a book, you can find almost anything. Open your laptop and start searching, and you'll find plenty of options.

This fifth and final step to making yourself ready to begin homeschooling is just a matter of narrowing down all your options into a selection that fits your child's needs, household budget, and space allotment. And while there is no end to the options to choose from, most all curriculum falls into one of 5 major categories; Traditional, Programmed, Online, Unit Study, and Classical.

Traditional

A traditional curriculum is comprised of familiar textbook/workbook elements. They use a different book for unrelated subjects, and the books are typically organized to be age/grade specific. These types of curricula do well to cover the basics of every subject and typically included well-planned lessons. Their exhaustive teacher manuals offer maximum teaching security and are often preferred for first-time homeschooling parents. Traditional curricula can also be a good fit if your child is a visual or auditory learner. Kids who thrive on methodical routines similar to what you might find in a classroom setting, often enjoy traditional curricula.

Traditional curricula can be slightly cumbersome if you are juggling multiple ages/stages simultaneously, and with each subject needing its own set of books, the cost can sometimes be prohibitive.

Programmed

Programmed curricula require almost no parental involvement whatsoever. They tend to be self-paced, sequential, and are almost always very easy to use. The lessons are planned out by the program itself, and they tend to be thorough in most major content areas. Busy parents who work from home tend to lean on programmed curricula to make sure their child's educational basics are covered. Many families who are seasoned homeschoolers might lean into a year of programmed curricula if they have big life changes coming like a large family move or a new baby on the way.

While not a good fit for younger students or auditory learners, kids who thrive on routine, workbooks, and self-discipline will do well with programmed curricula.

Online

Online-based technological learning is a growing set of curricula that includes both Internet and software-based programs. The tech setting allows for interactive learning utilizing a broad multimedia approach, making it ideal for both visual and auditory learners. The tech setting creates the feeling of a more controlled environment and provides a structure that lets kids work independently. Some programs offer multiple teachers online for different classes, and kids can sometimes have virtual classmates.

They may require a little technological savvy as well as typing and reading skills, which could be a challenge in younger ages. Some have scheduled deadlines that do not allow for scheduling flexibility, and they can be "busy work" intensive if modeled after a schoolroom environment. These curricula can become cost-prohibitive when considering the program cost combined with the need for computers, laptops, headphones, etc.

Unit Study

Unit Studies offer a thematic approach to teaching that allows you to carve out niches based on child interest or seasons. They are set-up with most major subjects included within a particular topic, theme, historical era, etc. The unit study approach is favored by families who have kids in multiple ages/stages, all learning at the same time. Most unit studies use living books versus textbooks, and you can easily switch units as frequently as your child's interests change. Unit Studies are ideal for hands-on, multi-sensory learning.

Unit studies are fairly inexpensive to use, but they can have gaps where you would have to supplement missing core subjects like math or writing. As engaging as Unit Studies are, they can be overwhelming to new homeschool families as the plans are loose, increasing parental structure dependency. Most unit studies offer the basic spine of the course, but it's up to the parents to acquire materials, books, and supplemental math or other core curriculum, etc.

Classical

Classical curricula uses the trivium to approach education based on the three ways children learn as they grow and develop; grammar stage from preK-3rd grade, the dialectic stage from 3rd to 6th grade, and rhetoric stage from 6th grade to adulthood. Classical-style curricula is preferred by families with children close in ability level. It leans heavily on real books and integrates unit studies in for topical content. The progression of knowledge is systematic, placing hooks of memory work in the early years that children unpack as they get older.

Because of its three-stage approach, multi-sensory learners do well with classical curricula. The classical approach can sometimes feel unstructured when looking at short-term goals. Parents are dependent on organizing resources and schedules a little more, and there is a risk of missing specific skills for kids if not well organized. Parent education, and reeducation, is necessary to help avoid educational gaps.

A note of caution.

Once you start shopping, the options are endless, and it can feel overwhelming. Many first-time homeschoolers get entirely lost in the sea of possibilities and begin to doubt their ability to make a wise choice. So, break it down into smaller steps, to make it a more manageable flow of information. Take into account your previous steps and use them to help you narrow your search.

For example, my reason for homeschooling was to afford our family the flexibility to balance my son's medical appointments and needs. So, for us, the online/technology-based curricula became a non-starter due to the rigid nature of their scheduling demands. My search pool narrowed to just four categories. Over time I learned that I have three kids with three different learning styles, and none of them were auditory. My kids need to see and touch and feel their education with reckless abandon; thus, the Programmed form of curricula was out of the running leaving me just 3 categories to look at.

You can use this same approach with your own family to help you narrow your search into a category of educational resources that you think will fit your family best *at this time*. Then do a search based on that to get a preliminary list. With that list, take your space and budget into account to narrow the field even further until you have a shortlist of options to compare, contrast, and ultimately make the plunge.

And remember, curriculum is the great equalizer. Don't let your own doubts derail your efforts and don't allow comparison to steal your joy. Should a curriculum choice you select today turn out not to be a good fit, sell the used materials to redeem some of your cost outlay and move forward to a new selection. Embrace the wide variety available to you and enjoy the process of learning new things!

FAQ's

When contemplating all the questions I get asked over the years as a homeschooler, this first question rises quickly to the top of the heap. This little chestnut is tossed around so freely that seasoned homeschoolers cringe at the very mention of the word.

What about socialization?

This question is asked mostly by nosy passersby or extended family, and quite often it's uttered with a whiff of disdain or pity for a life-time of isolation. Reality is, the opposite is true. Homeschooling is an open-door to more freedom than most can imagine. Most homeschool kids are as equally comfortable engaging with adults as they are their peers. Homeschoolers can play with older kids, as well as younger kids. Different disabilities are as accepted as are differing religions, genders, and educational levels. Homeschool kids are rarely ever stuck sitting in a desk for hours on end, facing the front of a room, unable to speak without raising their hands. Homeschool kids are almost always full family units who interact daily, discussing their educational and family needs. So, imagine what a playgroup looks like. It's quite common that as few as three homeschooling parents can decide to meet up and share as many as nine or more kids. Add a group activity or 2 each week and most homeschool kids interact with a massive variety of people. Most parent's I know lament being in the car 5+ days a week!

Still, the question persists so much that it is researched by countless experts in the fields of early childhood education, childhood development, and even educational lawmakers. One such study published in 1986 by J.W. Taylor[20] concluded that homeschooled children were more socially mature than public school peers of the same age based on their continual practice at

---

[20] Taylor, John W., "Self-Concept In Home Schooled Children," 1986

mixed-age engagement. Another study commissioned by Discovery Institute[21] concluded that homeschooled children had fewer behavior problems than their counterparts, theorized to be due to constant exposure to a variety of problem-solving practices. In 2012, Peabody researcher Joseph Murphy wrote a book called *Homeschooling in America; Capturing and Assessing the Movement*[22]. The book was the result of a three-year-study into home education, where he provided an exhaustive history of the movement as well as demographic insights. He completely disposed of the socialization concern when he found that homeschoolers had vibrant social networks. Specifically, he stated, "Homeschoolers are successful and they don't perform worse than other students or seem to be disadvantaged in any way...if you have one teacher dedicated to one or two children, it's a success equation and so it doesn't surprise me that home education works." Homeschool children have been found to have a stronger

---

[21] Lines, Dr. Patricia -,*https://www.discovery.org/a/1068*

[22] Murphy, Joseph (2014) - *Homeschooling in America; Capturing and Assessing the Movement.* ISBN-10 9781626365681

connection[23] to their family's religious values, maintain higher self-concept awareness, and score higher on the Piers-Harris Children's Self-Concept Scale.

Socialization is the activity of mixing socially with others. Homeschoolers not only mix socially with others but *thriving* at it. If you do find a random homeschooler who you feel isn't well adjusted, I would remind you that you could just as easily find that same behavior pattern in a child within the traditional school system.

---

[23] Gen2 Survey by Dr. Brian Ray, president of National Home Education Research Institute.

Many parents who enter the homeschooling arena aren't ready to think long-haul. But some come to it late in the game, pulling their child from middle school and diving into the deep waters of high-school homeschooling. Their first, most prominent, question is always the same.

Can a homeschooler get into college?

The short answer to this is, yes! Home educated kids are not only welcomed but sometimes encouraged to apply at colleges from local community up to Ivy League Universities. In fact, many accredited universities seek out homeschoolers to boost enrollment numbers due to a high success rate. Homeschoolers have access to scholarships, financial aid, and just about any other financial assistance available to public/private school students.

Best part yet, because of the very nature of homeschooling's personalized curriculum approach, the transition to college is almost seamless, making kids primed for post-secondary degrees. Homeschoolers naturally have a large pool of educational opportunities and are exposed to a wide variety of cultures, backgrounds, histories, and more. Furthermore, homeschool kids are encouraged to develop a sense of self-directed learning that makes them well suited to university life's independent study requirements.

A news story[24] in 2018 found that the admissions process can sometimes look cumbersome, but the acceptance rate is not diminished in any way by having a homeschool transcript. Another report[25] quoted Michael Cogan, then director of institutional research and analysis at the University of St. Thomas. He found that homeschooled students earned higher SAT and ACT scores[26], earned more college credits prior to freshmen year, earned a higher-grade point average their first semester in college, and held a higher graduation rate than their peers. It's worth noting that homeschoolers were also found to be more socially engaged and

---

[24] _https://www.usnews.com/education/best-colleges/articles/2018-07-18/how-home-schooling-affects-college-admissions_

[25] _https://www.cbsnews.com/news/can-homeschoolers-do-well-in-college/_

[26] _Research Facts on Homeschooling -_ March 23, 2020 - Brian D. Ray, Ph.D. - National Home Education Research Institute.

participatory in voting and community service as well...but I digress.

Top schools like Harvard, MIT, Duke, Yale, and more, actively recruit homeschoolers. So much so that they often adjust their admissions policies to be more homeschool-friendly, some accepting portfolios of work over paper transcripts. In a highly competitive admissions situation, homeschoolers often have an advantage because some of them come to the table already holding college credits thanks to dual enrollment options. While the burden of good record keeping lands on homeschool parents, the payoff is worth the extra work. And if standardized testing results are needed, there are SAT, ACT, LSAT, and FairTest options open to all homeschool children. A great book on the subject is, And What About College[27], by Cafi Cohen.

---

[27] Cohen, Cafi (2000) - *And What About College.*
ISBN-10 0913677116

Families fall into the decision to homeschool for any number of reasons, from individual child health to whole family necessity. Because of the advantages homeschooling offers it's possible that single-parent households, or double-income families with two working parents, might consider home education.

Can we homeschool and still work?

Again, the short answer here is, yes. Homeschooling doesn't require as much hourly time as traditional schooling does. Most of us aren't dealing with upwards of 30 kids in a room, and there is no need for busywork or passing out materials, etc. Plus, kids can pretty much escort themselves to the bathroom or kitchen without the need for a full room line-up, bell system, and hall monitor. As such, you can pack a lot of good education into a relatively small but well-organized timeframe. This includes organizing assignments for your child when they are away[28] from you, or even embracing the fun of homeschooling in the evenings and on

---

[28] *Homeschooling When Your Child Is Away From You.* 2017 - Michelle Cannon.

weekends. As discussed in Step 1, when you defined your 'why', you will need to consider your family's finances. When you look at keeping things legal in Step 2, part of that will require you to make sure your child has safe care if you work outside the home. If you work in the house, you'll need to make sure your space in Step 3 leaves your child room to learn and a place for you to work successfully. And choosing the curriculum in Step 5 will be shaped by the amount of time you can invest in while working to maintain your mental health and the work/school/parenting balance.

If you are a single parent, it will be crucial that you invest time in Step 4. It would be best if you found a tribe that not only supports you emotionally, but that might be able to assist you physically too. You will have days of exhaustion, discouragement, loneliness, and frustration. Beyond that, you might have activities that require a pick-up or drop-off that you need to have covered by someone safe that you trust to keep your child on task and healthy when you are not around. Your support network will be clutch here.

You only have 24 hours in a day, and you will need peak time-management skills to make single-parent homeschooling successful. You will often need to learn to say no to good things to make time for the best things. You'll have to make sure you limit the extracurricular activities to make room for routine grocery shopping and errands. You will want to read a few books on organization and minimalist approaches to education. The overall opportunity cost[29] for activities will become your go-to bar for picking the best things to fill your days. Your new mantra will be Prioritize, Systematize, and Organize!

Double-income families will have a different set of challenges to consider. Resources might be a little more fluid, allowing for things like a live-in au pair or weekly house cleaning, but they'll have to juggle multiple work schedules and dueling work environments. You may need to alternate work shifts and enlist the help of trustworthy grandparents to fill gaps during the week.

---

[29] Tate, Mary Jo. (2014) *Flourish: A Balance for Homeschool Moms*
ISBN-10 194011036X

Curriculum choices from Step 5 will center around work your kids can do with as little lesson planning as possible.

The organization discussed in Step 3 will be more paramount in the family calendar than ever. Creating and sticking to a family calendar will help you know what to expect for the week. Parents can, and should, divvy up all responsibilities, including both homemaking and homeschooling. Leaving all of any one area to the sole responsibility of one parent can breed burn-out. Choosing the curriculum will become a team effort, and you might enjoy splitting the duties a little. If mom is great at math, and dad loves science, select your curriculum's accordingly and work the schedule around the off-times. You might need to set strict do-not-disturb times into your day to get work done, but that can be the time for reading and independent schoolwork.

In all cases, older kids can help with any littles you have running around and don't forget about the beauty of having kids learn "home ec" in a hands-on application with daily chores, cooking, and even yard work. Have a regular sports schedule?

Well that is now P.E. Need to have a family budget meeting? Welcome to real-world math! The greatest gift of homeschooling is the unbridled freedom to shape your child's optimal education around real-world applications that are available every day. Think outside the box and embrace the lifetime of learning your child will begin!

This next question seems to be uniquely limited to people shifting out of the public-school arena. Almost every single parent who has come to me for advice and insights on transitioning away from their school and into homeschooling inevitably comes around and asks.

How much does homeschooling cost?

Like any other part of child-raising, homeschooling has a multitude of things to factor in when discussing the cost. The bottom-line price is essential, but in reality, I believe what parents want is a list of things they'll have to buy. In general, the three primary areas where resources can be taxed are:

- Curriculum
- Supplies
- Extracurriculars

The curriculum we discussed in Step 5 is one of the most substantial items homeschooling parents buy. However, this can be as expensive or as cheap as you make it, and you get full control over your choices. Once you have narrowed down the type of curriculum you want to purchase, search for discounts or coupons.

Some curricula providers run annual or seasonal sales. Others have a "scratch and dent" section where they keep open boxes or returned curriculum that they sell at a discount. I once purchased our entire history curricula at 80% off just by calling and asking! If you need to keep it cheaper still, some online curriculum options are 100% free. Frankly, there is so much on the internet these days from social media connections, used curriculum resale groups, bloggers, and the like, that you can almost wholly stock a school space just in free printables and slightly used books. You might need to shell out a little more to accommodate any special needs or learning disabilities, but that might well be the case even if you had your kids in a traditional school setting and needed supplementation.

School supplies are the colorful shiny light I flock to each year and spend entirely too much on because I like pretty paper and feel the need to have all the pens and crayons. But the reality is your kid needs a pencil, paper, and maybe some colored pencils. Get thee to thy dollar store. You can stock a full house of basic art and school supplies for less than 20 bucks if you know when, where, and how to shop. Furthermore, during the back to school season, even Amazon[35] runs big-box sales on supply kits by grade that you can point, click, and ship for a fraction of the time you would spend drooling over matching folders (I seriously love school supplies) and coordinating post-its. It's also worth noting that while this is one of the items you will spend a little cheddar for to homeschool, you would be buying this if your child was in the public/private school system. So, this cost is not exclusive to homeschooling.

Extracurriculars are all items like art, music, sports, field trips, etc. While some school districts welcome homeschoolers to join in for these types of classes, it is rare. More often than not, homeschoolers participate in these classes online, in private tutor settings, or via the local town programs. The costs can vary in range from minimal to expensive, and again, you get to control the price on what you choose to select. There are a ton of online options for art, music, and more that allow your child to get basic

---

[35] Amazon - *Ready for School.*

instruction and exposure to different opportunities from the comfort and safety of your home. At that point, your only cost would be supplies and, again, this is something you would likely have to purchase if you put your child in public school as well.

Some people like to harp on the hidden costs of homeschooling, like some villain in your favorite book, but I don't see the numbers to support this assumption. Sure, homeschoolers have gas costs for field trips and outings, but frankly you'd be spending that gas money each day sitting in the pick-up line for school. Yes, there will be a slight increase in your grocery bill with your child being home during the day, but it's easily offset in the savings you will find skipping back-to-school clothes shopping or replacing back-packs and homeroom supplies mid-year.

One of the best things I can tell you is not to get too worried about that kind of tiny nickel and dime stuff. If you put pen to paper and can afford your basics, you can make homeschooling work. You can find curricula free or cheap if you have a good network of parents to share with. You can get supplies inexpensively, and the library just became your best source of free reading and curriculum material.

The toughest question I face, by far, is the one coming out of the mouth of a parent who is already taking on the herculean task of championing for their child with special needs. So, to you, I want to say, I see the exhaustion behind your proud cape, and I'm here to help answer this very precious question.

Can I homeschool my special needs child?

I stumbled into homeschooling after embracing the reality that the school schedule and system weren't a great fit to accommodate my child's health conditions. My oldest son has Type 1 Diabetes, Celiacs, and Immuno-Globulin A Deficiency. Any one of these on their own might have been manageable, or even two, but all three combined makes for a storm in his body. His health requires constant, 24/7/365 monitoring to make sure he's healthy and safe. I never doubted the school system would do their very best; I just knew I would do better as his mother. So, as they say, the rest is history.

Every single child is special from their adorable freckled nose to their teeniest pinky toes. But if you have one of the extra special jewels that is medically complex, has neurological challenges, or is outside of the typical definition of developmentally ordinary, I'm here to tell you, yes…you can homeschool your precious baby. Not only is it possible, but in some cases, it's ideal since public schools come with the usual mix of sights, sounds, smells, and stimulations that can make processing hard for some of our mightiest warriors. You *can* homeschool your child with special needs; however, it will look a little different.

Adding in the educational component can feel overwhelming to a parent who is already fairly overwhelmed. So, start slow and easy. Take that curriculum Step 5 and weed out any curricula that require intense lesson planning. You might need shorter lessons, untimed testing, and extra accommodations for reading or writing. Search for curricula catered to your child's need (there are so many options I couldn't begin to list them all) and build around that. Keep your actual curricula load light the first year, focusing only on the core subjects, and leave lots of time for you and your child to adjust to the new schedule.

Know that you have the ultimate flexibility to accommodate doctor and specialist visits, and you can do a lot of learning on the road via audiobooks. Don't hold yourself to any hard and fast schedule beyond daily learning. Let your child's natural learning pace guide you so that you both enjoy the process. Encourage them to become active learners through exploration and discovery. Embrace that they may zoom ahead in one subject and need lots of help in another. The freedom of homeschooling is the perfect way to balance this kind of chaos.

Your driving reason might be plainly before you, but once you begin contemplating Step 3, your space requirements will need to account for different things. Perhaps you need a therapy corner for in-home PT, OT, VT, or any other alphabet soup of specialists. Maybe you need a supply closet for medical needs, or an extra fridge in the laundry room to hold formula, medications, and equipment. If your child needs extra services, you must find those resources so make sure you account for the daily space needed.

Invest in time drafting up a plan for you, the parent, to have some space too. While your child might be thriving in an environment perfectly individualized to meet their needs, you will need to carve out some mental space to make sure you are balanced.

That tribe I discussed in Step 4 will be absolutely necessary. Find and connect with other homeschool moms rocking the special needs super-capes. You'll need to have someone who understands more about your daily challenges, and having that soundboard can be like oxygen on days when things feel heavy. If you can't find homeschooling parents that match your situation, look for support groups or even faith-based parent organizations.

> Build a support net, embrace your child's unique learning needs, and dive-in to homeschooling!

You are *already* doing a fantastic job for your child, and you will undoubtedly double-down on all that awesomeness when you dive into homeschooling.

Final Thoughts

My advice herein would be completely hypocritical if I didn't fully own that I am merely a mom who fell into homeschooling out of necessity. I am not a degreed educator, nor am I an oft-lauded pillar of knowledge with authoritative letters behind my name. I am, however, in my prime, and with age comes experience and the wisdom that can only be gained through glorious failure. I have tried to rise above my shortcomings and learn to do better, and now hope to share my knowledge with you.

I don't have any bitterness against traditional school systems or the angels who work within them. I simply love my homeschooling life and the friends with which I share my home education journey. This book is fully born from a deep desire to help the world understand homeschooling a little better. It's meant to help facilitate thoughtful dialogue. My greatest hope is that new homeschooling parents can feel empowered just as much as a non-homeschooling parent can read this and enjoy a few A-HA moments of enlightenment.

Homeschooling, like every single iota of parenting, is a choice we are free to make but not always one easily done. For me, when at last my long-feared declaration of homeschooling came blabbering out of me, it was less a confident declaration and more a cry for help. I never envisioned my parenting journey would include homeschooling. The same is true for many parents who are making this same weighty choice today.

Whether you look at the decision to homeschool as brave or weird, make no mistake that when push comes to shove and your child needs it, you can do it. The transition might be rough, the learning curve steep, but never doubt yourself in your own ability to rise up and meet the needs of your family in whatever form that may present itself.

I hope these first steps, help you take the most exciting step ever.

Welcome to Homeschooling.

Resources & SUPPORT

BOOKS

102 Picks for Homeschool Curriculum, The - Duffy, Cathy (2014).

Better Together - Barnhill, Pam (2018)

Brave Learner, The - Bogart, Julie (2019)

Call of the Wild and Free – Ainsley Arment (2019)

Homeschool Bravely - Erickson, Jamie (2019)

Homeschooling 101 - Arndt, Erica (2013)

Honey for a Child's Heart – Gladys Hunt (2002)

Love The Journey - Somerville, Marcia (2014)

Read-Aloud Family, The – Sarah Mackenzie (2018)

Teaching From Rest - Mackenzie, Sarah (2015)

Unhurried Homeschooler, The - Wilson, Durenda (2016)

Well-Trained Mind, The - Wise, Susan (2016)

A few of my favorite things...

Easy Organization w/ Rolling Drawer Cart – 15 drawers, handy top shelf and wheels to let it roll anywhere you need to keep your space tidy.

All My Favorite Brands for pens, pencils, paper, and more.
- Pilot brand Frixion Pens.
- Ticonderoga brand Pencils.
- Five Star brand Paper.
- Crayola brand everything!

The best paper planners I've found for organizing all our lessons & activities and teaching my kids to manage their own time better.
- Erin Condren Teacher Planner
- Blue Sky Academic Planner.

Websites

Cathy Duffy Reviews – Amazing Homeschool Curricula Reviews- https://cathyduffyreviews.com/#

Homeschool Buyers Co-op - world's largest buyers' club for homeschooling families. - https://www.homeschoolbuyersco-op.org/

Rainbow Resource Center – The giant one-stop-shop online superstore of homeschool curriculum. - https://www.rainbowresource.com/

Legal Resources

Homeschool Legal Defense Assoc. (HSLDA) - https://hslda.org/

"We've made it our goal to tirelessly advocate for the right to homeschool—in courts, legislatures, & anywhere else we can make ourselves heard. Ultimately, we're here to empower & encourage homeschooling parents as they seek to teach their children in a way that celebrates their uniqueness & nurtures their love of learning. In short, our mission is to make homeschooling possible."

Nat;l Home Ed. Research Inst. (NHERI) - https://www.nheri.org/

"The institute has hundreds of research works documented & catalogued on home schooling, many of which were done by NHERI. Simply put, NHERI specializes in homeschool research, facts, statistics, scholarly articles, & information."

Homeschool State Laws - https://homeschoolstatelaws.com/

An easy to read starting point of homeschool laws for all 50 states

ABOUT THE AUTHOR

Heather D. Nelson is, first and foremost, a wife and a mom. When not writing, blogging, or advocating for her son with Type 1 Diabetes, she is busy homeschooling all three of her sons.

Writing began as a healing outlet for her and evolved into a full-blown career in 2009. Since then she has gone on to publish several non-fiction books, freelances as a brand journalist, and is soon jumping into the Fiction realm. She adores telling stories and using those to encourage others. She lives for love and laughter and all the joy she can squeeze out of her messy, sloppy, loud, crazy, amazing life.

STAY CONNECTED
www.heatherdnelson.com
twitter /instagram /pinterest
@LegitHDNelson

Other Books by Heather D. Nelson

Hail Mary for Peanut

Sometimes, the road to a family doesn't go as planned. Dreams for a baby are all too often waylaid by infertility, miscarriage, pregnancy loss, and more. Those unexpected hurdles can create strife in a marriage and even a trial to one's faith and the wake of it all can leave most couples struggling to hold onto hope.

In Hail Mary for Peanut Heather shares her emotional journey to parenthood after it's discovered that all her dreams and plans have gone awry. She shares all the raw ups and downs of her own story, while infusing each chapter with wit, wisdom, and genuine concern for others. She even includes a section of practical tips for coping with the stress of infertility and pregnancy loss both for the couples in the battle, and the family and friends on the sidelines.

This book is timely for any couple of faith encountering struggles in their family planning making this a perfect one-stop-shop for support and encouragement.

Publication Date: 07-04-2018
ISBN-10: 1979249407
ISBN-13: 978-1979249409

Available in paperback and ebook on
Amazon & Barnes & Noble.

Other Books by Heather D. Nelson

Just Stop: 10 Things Everyone Should Stop Saying

Do you ever really pay attention to some of the casual phrases people throw around? Have you ever had someone toss a platitude your way during times of stress of chaos and thought to yourself 'this is not helping me'? Then THIS is the book for you!

Recipient of the Readers' Favorite 5 Star Award, *Just Stop: 10 Things Everyone Should Stop Saying* is a collection of essays about some of the most commonly used phrases in today's society.

Heather D. Nelson discusses why flippant delivery can quickly become errant receipt. Start reading, and learn how to avoid these common communication pitfalls. Improve your capacity for human connection and become a more compassionate person. Better yet, buy a set to hand out at the office or gift to friends and family to stimulate great conversation.

Publication Date: 08-21-2018
ISBN-10: 1724880896
ISBN-13: 978-1724880895

Available in paperback and ebook on
Amazon & Barnes & Noble.

Out of print:
God Had Other Plans